Two Magpies

THE A–Z OF HOMEMADE JELLIES & JAMS

THE A-Z OF HOMEMADE JELLIES & JAMS

Words by Amelia Carruthers
Illustrations and Design by Zoë Horn Haywood

CONTENTS

Introduction 1

General Preliminaries 3

Recipes 5

    A is for. . . Apple 6

    B is for. . . Blackberries 8

    C is for. . . Currants 10

    D is for. . . Damsons 12

    E is for. . . Elderflowers 14

    F is for. . . Figs 16

    G is for. . . Ginger 18

    H is for. . . Herbs 20

    I is for. . . Ingredients 22

    J is for. . . Jars 25

    K is for. . . Kiwi 26

    L is for. . . Lavender 28

    M is for. . . Mint 30

    N is for. . . Nectarines 32

    O is for. . . Oranges 34

CONTENTS

P is for... Pineapples 36

Q is for... Quince 38

R is for... Roses 40

S is for... Strawberries 42

T is for... Temperature 45

V is for... Vanilla 48

W is for... Walnuts 50

X is for... Xmas! 52

Y is for... Yuletide 54

Z is for... Zest 56

Serving Suggestions 59

Ten Top Tips and Tricks 61

INTRODUCTION

Welcome to the wonderful world of jellies and jams.

As well as lots of classic recipes, this book is filled with tips and techniques on making the perfect preserve. What's more, you don't even need lots of equipment or a vast array of ingredients to get started. Making your own jams and jellies at home is very often cheaper than buying them - perfect for the thrifty home-chef. The cost of ingredients is low (especially if you pick them yourself), and by creating large batches, you can save a huge amount of money.

Preserving fruit by turning it into jam, for example, involves boiling (to reduce the fruit's moisture content and to kill bacteria, yeasts, etc.), sugaring (to prevent their re-growth) and sealing within an airtight jar (to prevent recontamination). Thats it! Jellies are largely similar, but generally involve the addition of gelatine and 'straining' to produce a clear end result. Such methods of preservation with the use of either honey or sugar was well known to the earliest cultures, and in ancient Greece, fruits kept in honey were common fare. Quince, mixed with honey, semi-dried and then packed tightly into jars was a particular speciality. This method was taken, and improved upon by the Romans, who *cooked* the quince and honey (similar to our modern jams)- producing a solidified texture which kept for much longer.

These techniques have remained popular into the modern age, especially so during the high-tide of imperialism, when trading between Europe, India and the Orient was at its peak. This fervour for trade had two fold consequences; the need to preserve a variety of goods, and the arrival of sugar cane in Europe. Preserving fruits through jams and jellies became especially popular in Northern European countries, where there was not enough natural sunlight to dry food outdoors. Jellies were a mainstay of the upper-class Victorian table, more used for decoration and display (some moulds were incredibly elaborate - almost pieces of art) than food preservation proper. Made in ceramic moulds, cut jelly shapes were suspended in clear jellies, and multi-part moulds allowed for centres with contrasting colours and flavours. Austerity in the war years soon put a stop to such complex production, but for the common people though, Jellies were most frequently used for savoury items. Some foods such as eels, naturally form a protein gel when cooked - and this dish became especially popular in the East End of London, where they were (and are) eaten with mashed potatoes. Not to worry though, in this *A-Z of Jams and Jellies* we'll be sticking strictly to fruits and flowers!

The wonderful thing about making your own homemade products is the fun one can have with creating customised labels and garnishes to the finished jars (think berries, citrus zest, herb sprigs) – a perfect present as well as personal treat. We hope that the reader is inspired by this book to start making their own jams and jellies, a delicious and rewarding pastime.

Amelia Carruthers

GENERAL PRELIMINARIES

Always ensure the fruits that you use in your jam or jelly recipes have been washed thoroughly, especially if they have been gathered from low hedgerows, or bushes that are near roads. If the fruits have pips or cores, you may wish to remove these before cooking, as some may leave a bitter taste to the final product. Some however, such as apple's pips, cores and peel contain vital pectin which will ensure your jam or jelly reaches a proper consistency. This does differ, so make sure to read each recipe carefully.

The recipes in this book will use either 500g or 1kg of fruit (if this is the main ingredient), which should produce between three and six traditional jam jars, or the equivalent of jelly. The amount of jam or jelly you produce will depend on how strong you wish the end result to be though. Some people prefer much thicker, viscous jams, whilst others will only be looking for a lightly flavoured jelly. Other ingredients such as lavender, rose or ginger will require much less 'primary ingredient' though, as their natural flavours are so strong. Have fun experimenting and just use what you've got!

Within this A-Z, you will find information on how to select your jam jars - as well as how to sterilise and seal them properly. You will also find essential tips on temperature (how to check a jam or jellies setting point), what equipment and utensils you will need, and how to select the best and freshest ingredients for your homemade treats. Good luck, and happy cooking.

RECIPES

A IS FOR... APPLE

Traditional folklore is brimming with references to the apple tree's virtues. This ancient, and thoroughly English tree has provided abundant food for centuries, and has many uses in the kitchen (both sweet and savoury) as well as herbal remedies. The crab apple (Pyrus Malus) is native to Britain, and is the wild ancestor of all our modern-day cultivated varieties. Today, most wild English varieties of crab apples are red in colour, meaning that your resultant jelly will have a beautiful, pale red sheen - not to mention plenty of flavour! Crab apples are ready for picking in late autumn, so this dish will make a perfect accompaniment to those warming-winter-roasts. Also, try this jelly as a glaze with smoked and cured meats as well as a wonderful addition to traditional gravy, giving a hint of fruit sweetness to your dishes.

Crab Apple Jelly

Ingredients

- 1 kg Crab Apples
- 250g Caster Sugar
- 1 Lemon

Method

1. Wash your apples and remove any bruised fruit (leaving this in would adversely affect the quality of the finished jelly).
2. Place the apples with enough water to cover in a saucepan.
3. Bring to the boil and cook until the fruit is soft (this should take roughly thirty minutes).
4. Pour the pulp into a jelly bag (over another saucepan) and let it strain overnight. Remember not to squeeze the bag, or this will make your jelly cloudy.
5. The next day, add the sugar in the ratio of ten parts juice, to seven of sugar. Also, add a good squeeze of lemon juice.
6. Bring to the boil, and stir to dissolve the sugar.
7. Keep at a rolling boil for roughly forty minutes, making sure to skim off any scum which rises to the surface.
8. Test the setting point (see the section on **T**emperature) – if your jelly is set, take it off the heat, if not, carry on cooking.
9. Pour your jelly into warm, sterilised jars and tightly seal. Voila!

B IS FOR...
BLACKBERRIES

Blackberries are wonderful little fruits, found all over England, most often growing wild in hedgerows. During the autumn months they are in abundance, so why not gather some up to make this delicious jam. Make sure you rinse the fruit thoroughly before you get started. This will be a delicious accompaniment to a pork roast - especially to give a fruity twist to a rich gravy.

It should be noted that generally, whatever jams you make - these can probably be made into jellies, and vice versa. Jam and Jelly making is a fun, and highly personalised business – so once you've got the basic techniques mastered, get creative!

Blackberry Jam

Ingredients

- 1kg Blackberries
- 900g Granulated Sugar
- Knob of Butter
- Squeeze of Lemon Juice

Method

1. Place the Blackberries into a heavy-bottomed saucepan, adding about 50ml of water and the lemon juice.
2. Bring to a slow boil, and cook the fruit for roughly fifteen minutes (or until soft)
3. Add the sugar and stir until completely dissolved.
4. Raise the heat and cook on a full boil for about ten minutes.
5. Check the setting point of your jam (see **T**emperature) – and if it wrinkles then it is finished cooking.
6. Remove the jam from the heat and skim off any scum which may have risen to the surface.
7. After this, stir a knob of butter across the surface, and this will also help to dissolve any remaining scum.
8. Allow to cool slightly, and pour into warmed, sterilised jars. Seal and Label.

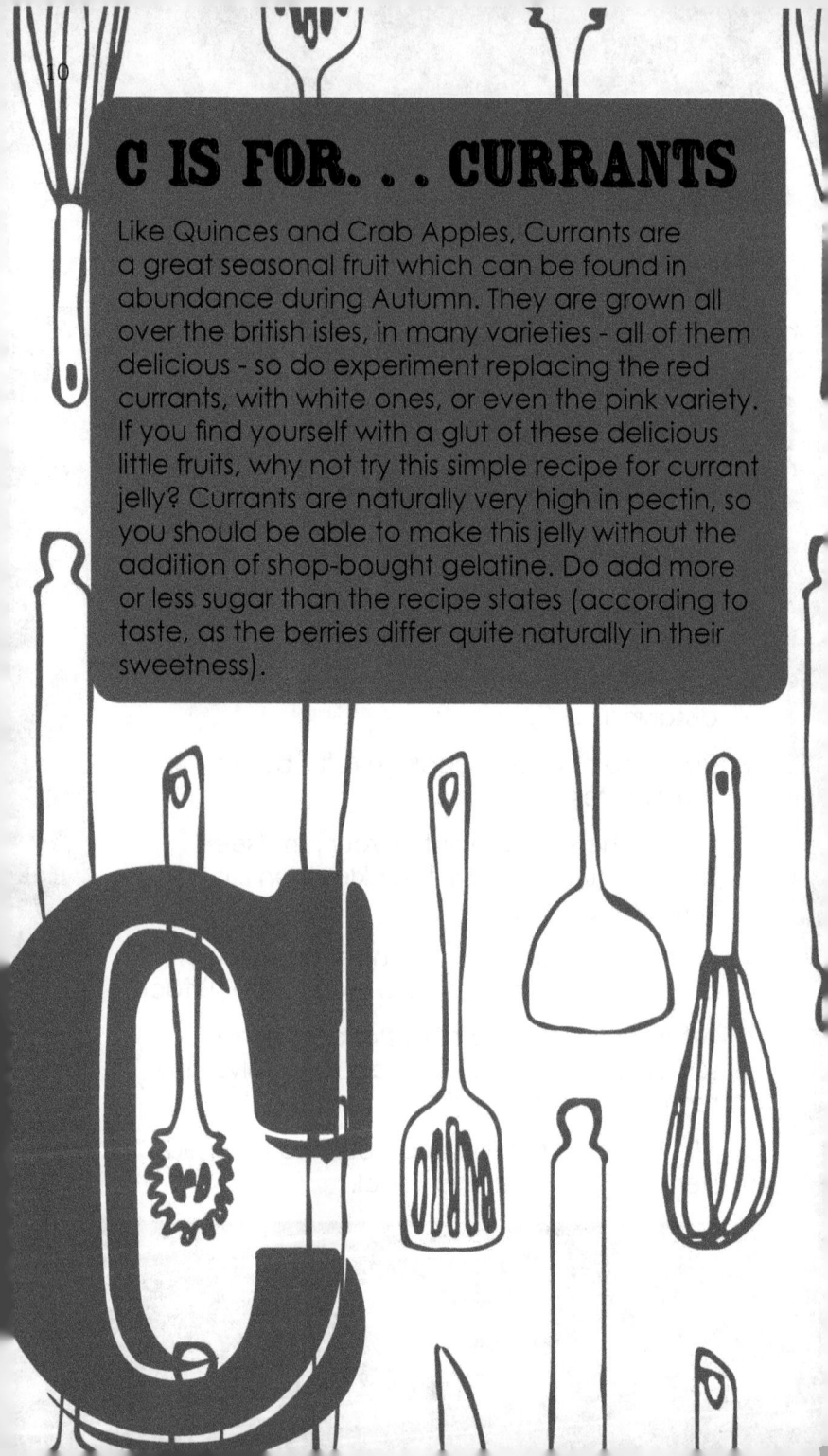

C IS FOR... CURRANTS

Like Quinces and Crab Apples, Currants are a great seasonal fruit which can be found in abundance during Autumn. They are grown all over the british isles, in many varieties - all of them delicious - so do experiment replacing the red currants, with white ones, or even the pink variety. If you find yourself with a glut of these delicious little fruits, why not try this simple recipe for currant jelly? Currants are naturally very high in pectin, so you should be able to make this jelly without the addition of shop-bought gelatine. Do add more or less sugar than the recipe states (according to taste, as the berries differ quite naturally in their sweetness).

Red Currant Jelly

Ingredients

- 1kg Currants
  (Red Currants are lovely ones to start with)
- 750g Granulated Sugar
- Water

Method

1. Place the (washed) currants – stalks and all, with a little splash of water in a heavy-bottomed saucepan.
2. Bring them slowly to the boil and as soon as the fruit is cooked (which will probably take about ten minutes) – add the sugar.
3. Bring the mixture up to a rapid boil for about eight minutes, and stir the fruit, pressing against the edges of the saucepan to release the juice.
4. Let the mixture cool slightly and then pour into a jelly straining bag. Let it drip through naturally if you want a completely clear jelly.
5. Pour this liquid into warm, sterilised jars – and garnish with some fresh berries for added effect.

D IS FOR... DAMSONS

Damsons have been in the British Isles for a very long time. One frequently stated theory is that they were first introduced by the Romans (from the city of Damascus), though this is highly debatable. What is for known is that the damson is a subspecies of the plum tree – prized for its rich yet astringent taste, making it perfect for jam-making, and varieties are now found all over Europe. The name 'damson' most commonly *only* refers to forms which are native to Great Britain though, they are slightly smaller and sweeter than the European variants. Here is a modern-twist on the traditional damson jam; a damson Jelly, which will be sure to impress. Happy foraging.

Damson Jelly

Ingredients

- 1kg Damsons
- 1 Lemon
- Granulated Sugar

Method

1. Wash the damsons, and add them to a large, heavy-bottomed sauce pan with the juice of the lemon, and about 250ml water.

2. Bring this all slowly to the boil, and simmer until the fruit is soft. This should take about thirty minutes – though you can test this by squeezing the damsons against the edge of the pan with a fork.

3. Pour this mixture into a jelly bag – set over another large saucepan or bowl to catch the juice. Remember not to squeeze the bag if you want a clear jelly. You may have to leave this overnight.

4. Now, measure the juice, and add one gram of sugar for every millilitre of juice produced.

5. Put the liquid and the sugar back on the heat and stir until the sugar has dissolved.

6. Then raise the heat and rapidly boil until the setting point is reached (see *Temperature*)

7. Pour your warm jelly into warm, sterilised jars and seal. Once cool, your damson jelly is ready.

E IS FOR...
ELDERFLOWERS

Elderflowers are the pretty white flowers of the elder tree. They have been used in cooking for centuries, appearing in abundance in the British hedgerows - and are believed to have a number of health benefits. There is a whole host of wonderful folklore surrounding this lovely tree, one such tale recounting that the most auspicious time to encounter faeries is underneath the elder on midsummer night's eve. Its still an important plant today, and one of the main health benefits of elderflowers are that they are antioxidants, cleansing the lymph glands and reducing susceptibility to many chronic (mostly age-related) conditions. Elderflowers are best gathered on a warm day (never when wet), just as the many tiny buds are beginning to open. Do remember to leave some flowers for elderberry picking later in the year though! This recipe for elderflower jelly is sweet yet subtly flavoured, and has a gentle, floral aroma.

Elderflower Jelly

Ingredients

- 3 Gelatine Leaves
- 75g Caster Sugar
- 150ml Elderflower Cordial
- 350 ml Water
- Elderflower heads (optional, for decoration)

Method

1. This recipe will be even better with homemade elderflower cordial, but the shop-bought versions will work just as well. It is a really simple cordial to make, though will need about a week to infuse - so prior preparation is key.
2. Soak the gelatine in cold water (until soft), then drain and squeeze out the excess water
3. Place the cordial (homemade or shop bought), water and sugar into a saucepan.
4. Just before it comes to the boil, remove from the heat and add the gelatine leaves. Stir until dissolved.
5. Add the fresh flowers if you have them.
6. Strain the mixture and allow to cool (in a bowl or jars of your choice).
7. Just as the jelly is beginning to set, try distributing the flowers more evenly. Once cold, your jelly is ready to eat!

F IS FOR... FIGS

Native to the Middle East and western Asia, the fig has been sought out and cultivated since ancient times, and is now widely grown throughout the temperate world, both for its fruit and as an ornamental plant. It was cultivated from Afghanistan to Portugal to India, but it was only in the fifteenth century that the fig made it to England though. It was such a success that in the sixteenth century, Cardinal Reginald Pole gave these trees pride of place at Lambeth Palace, London. When ripe, there is nothing better than a fresh fig. The fruit is rich and sweet but doesn't transport well (hence the need to be preserved), making it the perfect ingredient for jam-making!

Fig Jam

Ingredients

- 1kg Figs (roughly chopped)
- 500g Granulated Sugar
- 1 Cinnamon Stick
- 1 Lemon (rind and juice)

Method

1. Place the figs, sugar, cinnamon and lemon in a large bowl, and leave the flavours to infuse overnight.

2. The next day, transfer the mixture with a little liquid into a large, heavy-bottomed sauce pan and cook over a low temperature until the sugar is completely dissolved.

3. Keep the ingredients over a very low heat and cook for roughly forty minutes, or until they have turned a thick, 'jam-like' consistency. (The figs should be able to be mashed against the side of the pan with a fork).

4. Allow the jam to cool slightly, then pour it (still warm) into warm, sterilised glass jars.

5. Once cold, your jam is ready to eat – try with yoghurt and *Rose Jam* for a truly middle eastern feel.

G IS FOR... GINGER

The warm and spicy flavour of fresh ginger makes a wonderful jelly, and is a very versatile ingredient to have stocked in your store cupboard. From its origin to the present, ginger is the world's most widely cultivated herb, but sadly, not as appreciated as it should be! Try this simple recipe for ginger jelly, which once made, can be added to an array of desserts and savoury asian dishes to really spice them up. Unlike most of the other recipes, you will not need that much ginger here, as the flavour is naturally very strong. Try with rhubarb for a light and refreshing summertime jelly, or with lemongrass and lime, as in this recipe - and serve with strawberries or even watermelon.

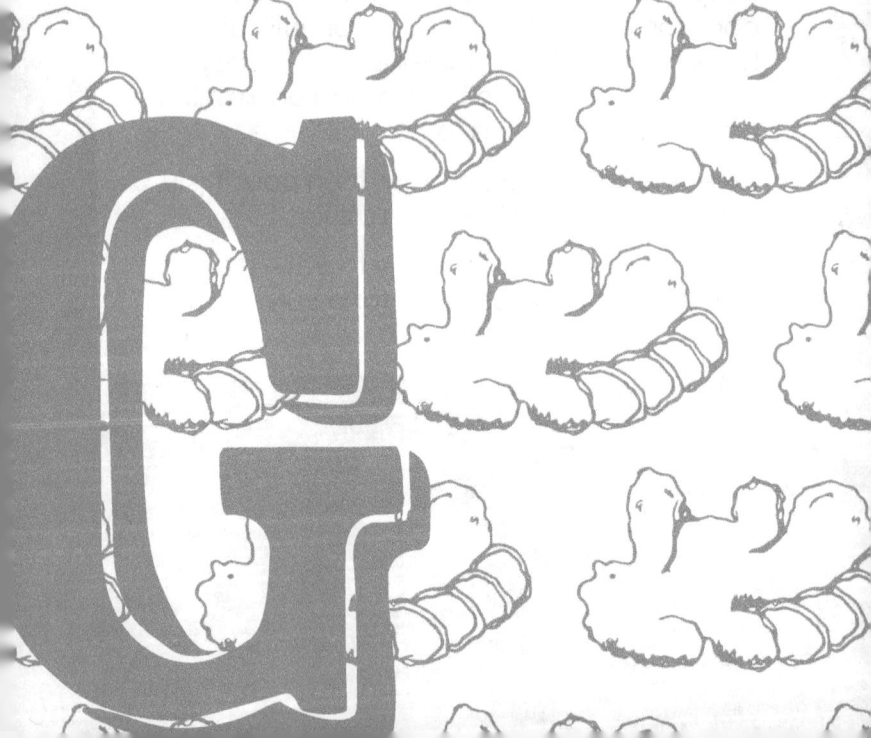

Ginger Jelly

Ingredients

- 3cm of sliced ginger
- 300g Caster Sugar
- 2 bruised lemongrass stalks
- 2 Limes (juice and zest)
- 3 Gelatine Leaves
- 850 ml Water

Method

1. Place the gelatine in a bowl of water, and soak until soft.
2. Place the lemongrass, ginger and lime zest in a heavy-bottomed saucepan with the water – and bring to the boil.
3. Once the mixture has boiled, take it off the heat and leave to cool.
4. Then, strain the liquid through muslin or a jelly bag and return to the heat.
5. Add the sugar and the gelatine (soft with the excess water squeezed out) and place over a very low heat – stirring constantly until everything is dissolved. Do not allow this to boil – if you do, the setting properties of the gelatine will not work.
6. Remove from the heat and add the lime juice.
7. Pour your warm jelly into warm, sterilised jars and seal. Serve with refreshing fruit on a summer's day!

H IS FOR... HERBS

Here, anything goes! The brilliant thing about making savoury herb jellies, is that you are in complete control of what you add into them. Once you have mastered the basic technique, you are in charge of the variations. Many herbs make great companions; rosemary and garlic with mint or parsley; fennel and marjoram with lemon thyme; or sage with tarragon. You should be aiming for is a sweet yet piquant jelly though - so think about the herbs you would like to see as accompaniments to your regular dishes. We particularly recommend this version of a classically English herb jelly; a combination of lemon thyme, rosemary and a hint of garlic, useful for livening stews, soups and gravies.

English Herb Jelly

Ingredients

- 1kg Cooking Apples
- 700ml Water
- 200ml wine or cider vinegar
- A sprig of Lemon Thyme
- A sprig of Rosemary
- 1 Large clove of Garlic
- 1 Lemon

Method

1. Cut up the apples (cores and skins included) and place them in a heavy-bottomed saucepan.

2. Add the bunches of thyme and rosemary (keeping some small leaves behind for decoration), the chopped garlic (here, feel free to add more or less according to taste) and the water.

3. Simmer with the lid on until the apples are soft (this should take about thirty minutes.)

4. Strain this mixture through a jelly bag over night, remembering not to squeeze it through if you would like a completely clear finished jelly.

5. Put this juice and the vinegar back in a heavy-bottomed saucepan and heat on a low temperature. Then add the sugar (in a ratio of 1g to 1ml of liquid) and stir until completely dissolved.

6. Bring the mixture to a rolling boil, add a good squeeze of lemon and after twenty minutes of cooking, test the setting point (see *T*emperature).

7. If your jelly has reached its setting point, take it off the heat.

8. Stir in the remaining small (or finely chopped) thyme and rosemary leaves once the jelly is partially setting.

9. Leave the jelly to cool slightly and pour into warm, sterilised jars. Once it is sufficiently cold and set – your jelly is ready for consumption!

I IS FOR...
INGREDIENTS

Sourcing your ingredients for jams and jellies is rather simple! All you will need are: sugar, pectinous or jelly producing bodies (usually homemade or shop bought pectin, or sheet gelatine), usually some form of citric acid, and the 'main ingredient' for your jam or jelly, whether that is a fruit, flower or herb.

Making your own jams and jellies is a fantastic way to use up surplus produce, much of which you may have grown yourself, or naturally foraged. Work out when fruits are in abundance, what time of year is best to pick them, and most importantly, *where* you can find them. In June, elderflowers are just coming out, whilst in July the currants make an appearance, followed by plums in September. For the more exotic jam or jelly though, as well as for necessary ingredients such as lemons, your local food-store should have everything you need.

Finding the best ingredients before you start cooking is important, as the better your initial ingredients are, the better the end-result will be. Look at the local produce on offer in your area. It is so often the case that the best things to eat are the things that grow locally, are in season, and haven't travelled a huge distance. Not only do these things taste better than their imported counterparts, but it is far kinder to the environment to use what is nearby. Perhaps you have a wonderful local greengrocer who can supply you with seasonal fruit, or a brilliant local health food shop where you can stock up on herbs and spices? Use your local suppliers and their expertise, as their knowledge will be rather useful to you while you are still getting to grips with the basics.

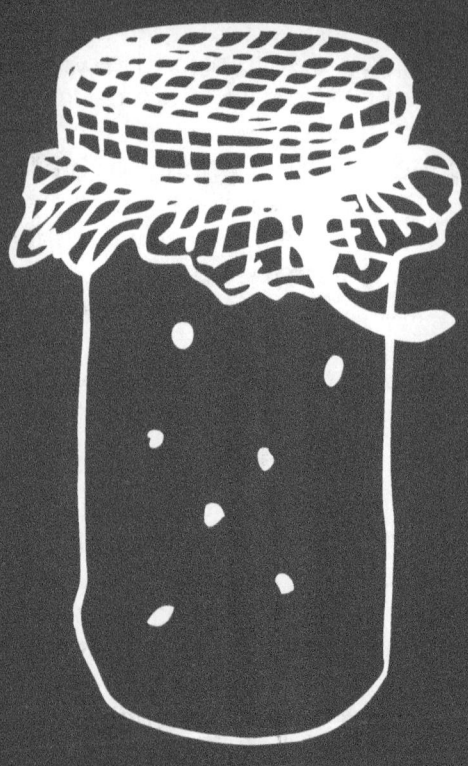

J IS FOR... JARS

Jam jars are very easy to come across, and should be sold at all local homeware stores as well as larger supermarkets. You should also try and buy some wax paper tops with which to seal them, if the lids are not airtight. There is really only one technique that you will need to master though, and that is: Sterilisation.

It is very important that you use sterilised jars to store your jam or jelly in, both during preparation and in the later stages of the process when you are storing your creations. This will help them to keep for longer, as it will remove any bacteria, yeasts or fungi and protect your liquids. Jars and that have not been sterilised properly will infect the food inside, meaning it will spoil very quickly and need to be thrown away. Sterilisation is a very simple process though, and can be done in a number of ways. The simplest way to sterilise your equipment at home is to wash the bottles or jars in very hot soapy water, rinse in more very hot water, and place them into an oven on the lowest setting (275°F/130°C/Gas 1) for twenty minutes. Ensure you use the bottles when they are still warm, and also that they are airtight when sealed to prevent bacteria entering the bottle.

N.B: Do not put cold liquids into hot jars, or hot liquids into cold jars; this may result in the glass shattering; a messy and dangerous problem to fix!

K IS FOR... KIWI

The kiwifruit has an incredibly interesting history. Initially known as the 'Chinese Gooseberry' (the fruit originated in Northern China) it is the edible berry of a woody vine. Cultivation of this fuzzy kiwifruit spread from China in the early twentieth century to New Zealand, where the first commercial plantings occurred. Here, the fruit was called 'yang tao' but was changed to 'Chinese Gooseberry' by the New Zealanders. It proved popular with American servicemen in New Zealand during World War II and after this, the fruit grew in worldwide popularity. Kiwis are naturally a little sour and have a beautiful, bright green colour. This unusual jelly will be sure to impress any visitors, and goes perfectly with lime.

Kiwi Jelly

Ingredients

- 1kg Chopped Kiwis (about 20 whole fruits)
- 100g Pectin
- 200ml Water
- 1 Lime

Method

1. Place the chopped kiwi in a bowl with about 200ml of water and bring to the boil.
2. Gently simmer for about five to ten minutes, then take off the heat.
3. Strain the mixture through a jelly bag (being careful not to squeeze it through if you want a clear jelly)
4. Combine the juice with the sugar and bring back to a gentle boil until the sugar has dissolved. Stir constantly.
5. Add the pectin and a healthy squeeze of lime juice and continue stirring. Then bring to a good boil for one minutes.
6. Allow the jelly to cool slightly, then place into warm, sterilised jars (or moulds if you prefer!).
7. Seal and store in the refrigerator – your jelly is ready to eat.

L IS FOR. . . LAVENDER

Lavender is a wonderful flower, famed for its aroma as well as its decorative uses. This recipe uses lavender blossoms - a truly fragrant and delicious way to enhance your jellies. When choosing your lavender use buts that have not opened and flowered completely, as the buds which are fully purple but still tightly wrapped will give the best aromatic qualities. They are highly elegant as well as edible, so why not try adorning your jelly with a sprig of lavender to finish. Try pairing your delicately flavoured jelly with dark chocolate for a truly stunning dessert. Do be careful not to use too much lavender in this jelly though; as it can very quickly become overpowering and overly fragrant.

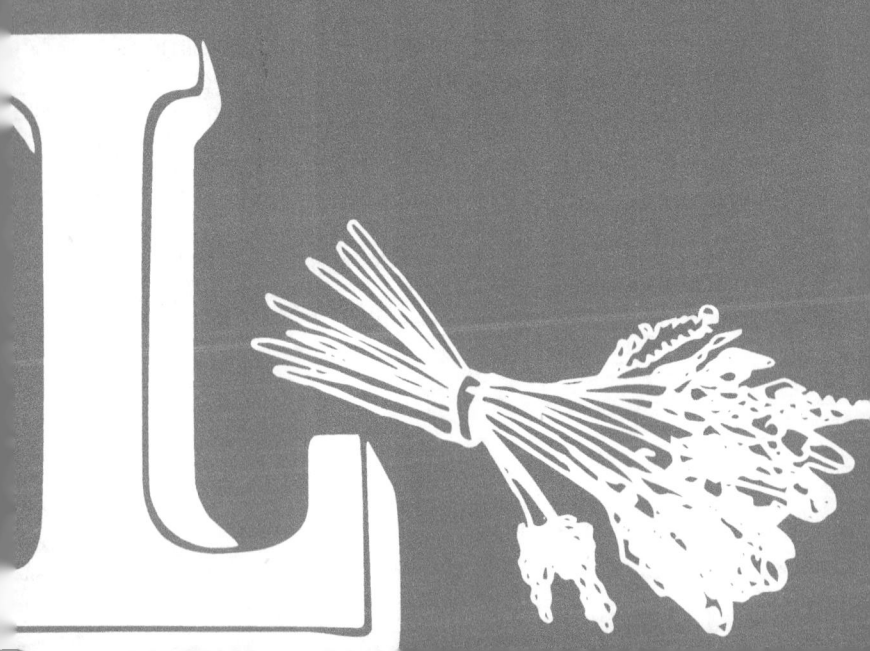

Lavender Jelly

Ingredients

- 100g Dried Lavender
- 800ml Water
- 850g Granulated Sugar
- 1 Lemon
- 4 Leaves of Gelatine

Method

1. Bring the water to the boil in a large, heavy-bottomed saucepan.
2. Remove it from the head and stir in the dried lavender flowers. Let this steep for twenty minutes.
3. Strain the mixture through a jelly bag into another saucepan.
4. Add the lemon juice and sugar and stir over a medium heat until the sugar has dissolved.
5. Then, take it off the heat and add the gelatine (previously soaked in water until soft) – stir until completely dissolved.
6. Transfer your warm jelly into warm, sterilised jars and seal. Once cool, it is ready to serve!

M IS FOR. . . MINT

Mint has a very long history, and has been used for its digestion-aiding properties for centuries. It is thought that mint was introduced to Great Britain by the romans, and was referred to by a John Gardiner in his *Feate of Gardening* (1440) as 'myntys.' It was not until the early sixteenth century however, that mint was used for sauces (especially the traditional combination with lamb) in England. But after this date, it's been popular ever since! The smell of mint is simply wonderful, as is its bright green colour, and it is just as good as a tea after dinner (just cut a few fresh leaves and pop them in a cup of boiling water). Here is a lovely recipe for a mint and apple jelly, perfect as an unusual yet delicious addition to your traditional Sunday Roast.

Mint Jelly

Ingredients

- 1kg Cooking Apples
- 20g sprig of Fresh Mint
- 50g finely chopped Mint Leaves
- 500ml Water
- 200ml wine or cider vinegar
- Caster Sugar (1g to 1ml of liquid produced)

Method

1. Cut up the apples (cores and skins included) and place them in a heavy-bottomed saucepan.

2. Add the sprig of mint and the water and simmer with the lid on until the apples are soft (this should take about thirty minutes.)

3. Strain this mixture through a jelly bag over night, remembering not to squeeze it through if you would like a completely clear finished jelly.

4. Put this juice and the vinegar back in a heavy-bottomed saucepan and heat on a low temperature. Then add the sugar (in a ratio of 1g to 1ml of liquid) and stir until completely dissolved.

5. Bring the mixture to a rolling boil and after twenty minutes of cooking, test the setting point (see *Temperature*).

6. If your jelly has reached its setting point, take it off the heat and stir in the remaining finely chopped mint.

7. Leave the jelly to cool slightly and pour into warm, sterilised jars. Once it is sufficiently cold and set – your jelly is ready for consumption!

N IS FOR...
NECTARINES

Nectarines are delicious stone fruits, similar to peaches but with a lovely smooth skin. Make sure to buy them when they are in season (and therefore cheaper). Making nectarine jam is the perfect way to preserve the juices of these fruits to enjoy at a later date. They are naturally sweet and would therefore be delicious with any manner of desserts; a gorgeous addition to pies, crumbles, and tarts. The combination of nectarine *and* plum is a fantastic one too, so why not try replacing half the nectarines with plums, for a truly exciting jam?

Nectarine Jam

Ingredients

- 1kg Nectarines (or 500g Nectarines, 500g Plums)
- 900g Golden Granulated Sugar
- Knob of Butter

Method

1. Place the Nectarines (chopped into chunks) into a heavy-bottomed saucepan.
2. Bring to a slow boil, and cook the fruit for roughly thirty minutes (or until soft)
3. Add the sugar and stir until completely dissolved.
4. Raise the heat and cook on a full boil for about ten minutes.
5. At this point, check the setting point of your jam (see *Temperature*) – and if it wrinkles then it is finished cooking.
6. Remove the jam from the heat and skim off any scum which may have risen to the surface.
7. After this, stir a knob of butter across the surface, and this will also help to dissolve any remaining scum.
8. Allow to cool slightly, and pour into warmed, sterilised jars. Seal and Label.

O IS FOR... ORANGES

Seville oranges are traditionally grown throughout the mediterranean region. They have thicker skin than their sweet counterparts as well as being higher in pectin - perfect for making homemade marmalades, and a great ingredient for the home-chef wishing to preserve a glut of seasonal produce. For your perusal, here we have a modern take on the traditional classic. If you are feeling particularly adventurous, try flavouring with dark muscovado sugar and a good dose of Scottish whisky for a truly grown up marmalade. Ginger is also a lovely addition.

Orange Marmalade

Ingredients

- 1kg Seville Oranges (unwaxed)
- 1.8 kg Granulated Sugar
- The Juice of 1-2 Lemons (according to taste)

Method

1. Wash the oranges and remove the top stalk.

2. Place them in a large saucepan with enough water to cover, and bring to the boil. You may need a heavy heat-proof plate to keep them submerged.

3. Simmer the oranges for two hours, or long enough so that the skins are soft (you can test by piercing them with a fork).

4. Take the oranges out the pan, preserving the liquid, and allow the fruits to cool.

5. Then, cut the oranges in half and remove the pips, pulp and pith– saving them for later, (trying to reserve the juice!) and cut the orange peel into strips – as thick or as thin as you like for the final marmalade.

6. Tie the pips, pith and pulp in a piece of muslin cloth.

7. Put all of this; orange juice, rind and sugar, along with about half the cooking liquid back into the saucepan and boil rapidly for about twenty minutes.

8. Test the setting point of your marmalade (see **T**emperature), and cook for longer if this point has not been reached.

9. When sufficiently cooked, allow the mixture to cool slightly, remove the bag of pips, and skim off any scum which has risen to the surface.

10. Pour it into warm, sterilised jars and seal. Your marmalade is ready.

P IS FOR...
PINEAPPLES

This recipe for spiced pineapple jam makes a wonderfully sweet yet flavoursome jam which is perfect for giving a tropical flair to any dish – sweet or savoury. It is a fantastic and thoroughly unusual spread on toast, as well as a lovely topping for ice creams - and even with a glazed ham. Pineapples have also been used in English kitchens for longer than you might think. There is infact a painting, created in 1675 by Hendrik Danckerts, which depicts Charles II being presented with the first pineapple grown in England. Because of their rarity, finding novel ways to preserve this delicious fruit was even more important, so why don't you have a go at this updated classic?

Spiced Pineapple Jam

Ingredients

- 500g Fresh Pineapple
- 500g Granulated Sugar
- 80g Pectin
- 1 Lemon
- 1 tsp ground Cinnamon
- ¼ tsp of ground Cloves
- 1 knob of Butter

Method

1. Place the pineapple (chopped), spices and the sugar in a heavy-bottomed saucepan and let it combine for one hour.

2. After one hour, place the pan over a medium heat and stir constantly until the sugar is completely dissolved.

3. Bring the heat up to a rolling boil, and cook for five minutes. Make sure to skim off any scum which rises to the surface.

4. After this, bring it down to a simmer and add the pectin – stirring constantly.

5. Bring back to a rolling boil for just one minute, then remove the pan from the heat, and again, skim any scum. If you stir a knob of butter across the surface, this will also help dissolving any remaining scum.

6. Let the jam cool slightly, then pour your warm jam into warm, sterilised jars and seal. Your tropical treat is ready.

Q IS FOR... QUINCE

Quince are small fruits which belong to the same family as pears - and a much under-used and under-appreciated British fruit. Quince trees are often grown for their pretty pink flowers, and the fruits are practically made for jams and preserves. They are grown all over England, and are a treat to find. Pick them in October or November, leaving to ripen in a cool place if necessary. Quince has an earthy flavour, almost a cross between an apple and a pear, and is commonly used as an accompaniment to cheese (making this jam a perfect accompaniment to a good cheese board).

Quince Jam

Ingredients

- 1 kg Quince
- 500g Granulated Sugar
- 1 Lemon

Method

1. Peel the quinces and remove the seeds. Cut them into small pieces and place in a bowl of water (to prevent browning).

2. Place the quince in a saucepan with just enough water to cover, and boil on a high heat for thirty minutes. They should be nice and soft.

3. Mash the quince with a fork until the mixture resembles a chunky applesauce.

4. Transfer back to a large saucepan and add the sugar, lemon and some more water (to get the appropriate 'jam' consistency). Cook for a further twenty minutes, stirring frequently.

5. Check the setting point (*see Temperature*) and if the jam is set, remove from the heat!

6. Transfer into warm, sterilised jars and seal. Over time the colour of your quince jam may darken – but this is completely natural.

R IS FOR... ROSES

Roses have a truly heady, delicious scent and in the British summer months, their blooms are everywhere. They are so pretty to look at, but are also great in cooking; used to great extent in Middle Eastern and Indian cuisines. Roses have also been used in English cooking since Tudor times (although they have since fallen out of fashion), but they have such varied uses – to scent honey, make sugared petals for cake decorations, additions to salads, or even... as rose petal jams! Rose jam is delicious served on top of yoghurt, with scones or muffins and as an elegant addition to homemade cakes or biscuits.

Rose Jam

Ingredients

- 500g of fresh rose petals
- 1 litre of water
- 500g of caster sugar
- The juice of 2 lemons

Method

1. Discard any rose petals with discoloration or imperfections – the colour of the rose petals will determine the final colour of your jam, so stick to single variety if you are aiming for a specific colour.

2. Place your rose petals in a bowl, and sprinkle sugar over them, making sure each petal is covered.

3. Leave these in the refrigerator for a few hours, for the flavours to infuse.

4. Place the remained of the sugar, the lemons and the water into a large, heavy-bottomed saucepan and cook on a low heat until all the sugar has dissolved.

5. Whilst the mixture is not-quite at boiling point, add the rose petals and sugar and keep on a medium heat, stirring constantly.

6. Let this simmer for about twenty minutes, then bring to a rolling boil for five minutes – or until setting point is reached.

7. Once the setting point has been reached (see, *T*emperature), take the jam off the heat and allow to cool slightly.

8. Put your warm jam into warm, sterilised glass jars and seal. This beautiful and fragrant jam is ready for consumption.

S IS FOR...
STRAWBERRIES

Here is a really simple recipe for a sweet and vibrant jelly. The strawberries have a lot of natural sweetness though, meaning that the sugar levels may have to be adjusted according to your own preferences. Scottish strawberries are especially famed for their wonderful taste, the colder climate doing these little fruits wonders - so try and source some if you can. Try mixing this jelly recipe with a hint of elderflower and sparkling wine - a delicious combination which will prove that strawberry jelly if for far more than children's parties...

Strawberry Jelly

Ingredients

- 1kg Strawberries
- 50g Caster Sugar
- 1 Lemon
- 4 Leaves Gelatine
- Elderflower or Sparkling Wine (optional!)

Method

1. If you are intending to present your jelly in moulds or jars, hold back some of these little fruits and place them in the containers. This will make a lovely finished presentation.

2. Place the gelatine leaves in a bowl of water until softened.

3. Place the strawberries, lemon juice, sugar – and either a little splash of water, elderflower cordial or wine, in a saucepan and heat on a low heat – until just simmering.

4. At this point, the choice is yours whether to strain the mixture or leave the strawberry pieces in. Leaving them in will give more flavour and texture to the jelly.

5. Take the pan off the heat and add the gelatine leaves (with the water squeezed out). Stir until combined, and add more liquid if required.

6. Once cool, pour the liquid into your jars or moulds – and decorate with fresh berries, or even elderflowers.

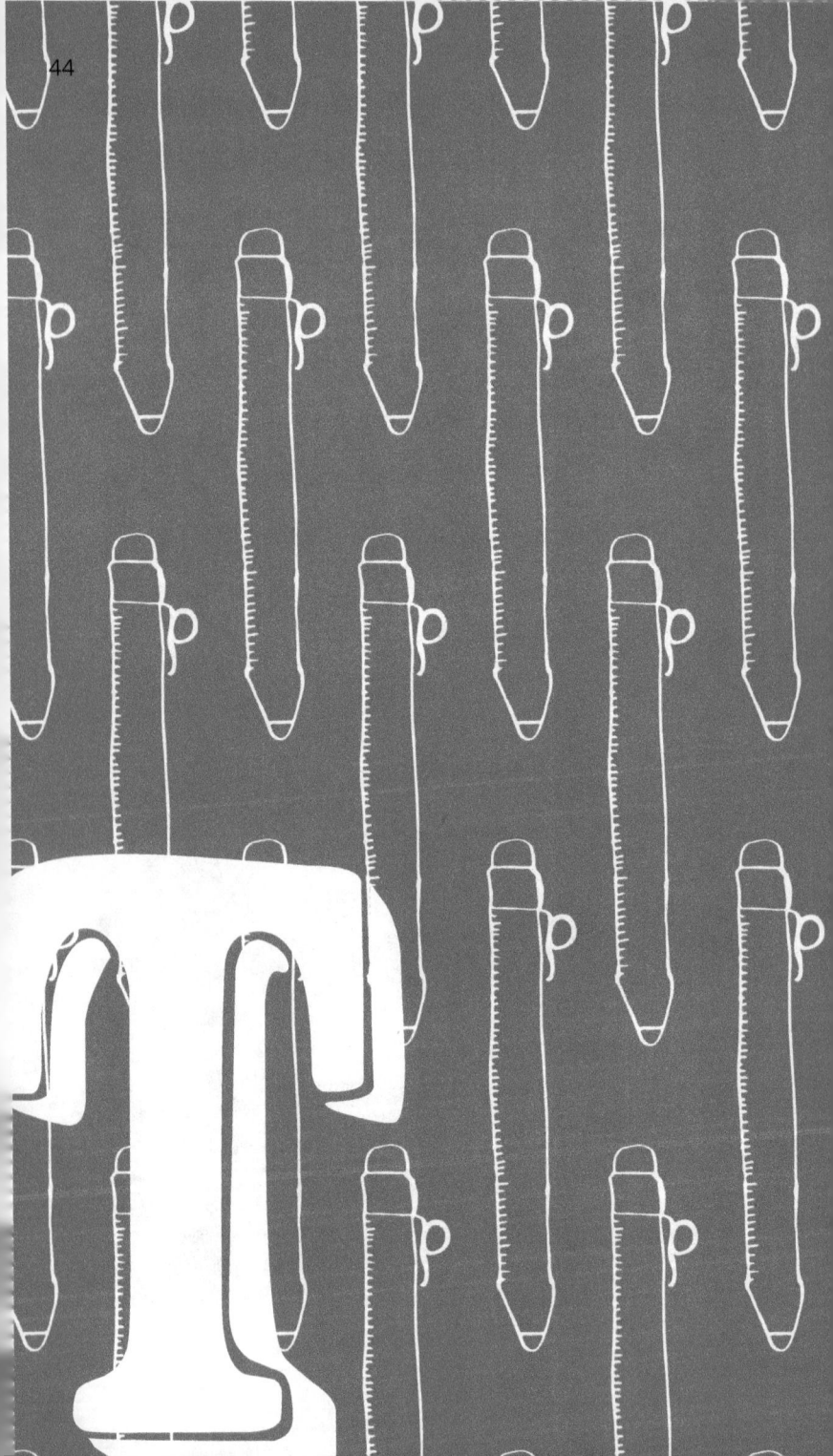

T IS FOR...
TEMPERATURE

As with any essential cooking skills, getting the temperature right is crucial! This is especially the case with jam and jelly making, and you will need to get to grips with 'Checking the Setting Point.' This is the point at which the mixture starts to set, and transforms from a fruit juice or puree into a jelly or a jam - magical!

Here's how to do it: Place a small plate or saucer into the fridge for roughly fifteen minutes - or until sufficiently cold. Pour a spoonful of the hot jam or jelly on to the plate and return to the fridge for about five minutes. Then, take it out and try pushing the edges of the jam with a spoon or a finger and if it is set, it will wrinkle slightly. Generally, follow the recipes advice on cooking / checking times - however, if your jam or jelly is not set, continue to check every five minutes. It is so important not to overcook - so be vigilant. A slightly 'looser' jam is preferable to one which has a burnt taste.

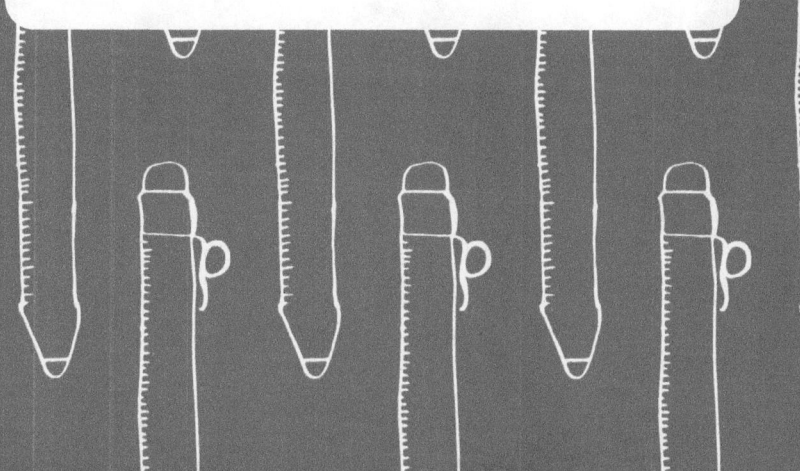

U IS FOR... UTENSILS

For the home jam and jelly maker, there is actually very little specialist equipment that you will need. The list of utensils and equipment is not huge, but it is important you have the basics at your fingertips. Your kitchen utensils are the tools of your trade, as it were, and you'll get the best results from your jam or jelly making if you take the time to source the right tools.

The equipment needed for jam and jelly making is rather basic, and you may already have most of it around the house. You will need saucepans, any earthenware or non-porous bowls and plenty of glass jam jars (for storing both jams and jellies; size and amount dependent on the batch size you are intending), as well as a 'jelly bag' for straining. When you have cooked the ingredients in a saucepan (heavy bottomed jam boilers work best), you may find it useful to purchase a stand or tripod, from which to leave the mixture to strain overnight. Though not essential, jelly moulds or decorated glass bowls will add a nice touch. Wooden spoons are great for stirring at high temperatures (as they do not conduct heat), and metal spoons are better for skimming off any scum which rises to the surface.

Check List:

- Saucepan (preferably heavy-bottomed)
- Bowls (for storing the fruit, or finished jelly)
- Large Spoons (wooden are the most useful)
- Sharp Knives (for chopping the fruit!)
- Jelly Bag (for straining)
- Glass Jars (for storage and presentation)

V IS FOR... VANILLA

This recipe makes for a really marvellous jam, using the classic English ingredient of Rhubarb, given a sweet and slightly musky flavour with the combination of vanilla. The addition of vanilla (a much underappreciated flavouring) will really enhance the natural tartness of the rhubarb. For this jam recipe to be at its best, vanilla pods really should be used, as the 'essence' simply doesn't have the same intensity of flavour. It will make a delicious addition to a traditional crumble, or even better - eaten on top of ice-cream or yoghurt. Enjoy.

Rhubarb and Vanilla Jam

Ingredients

- 1kg Rhubarb
- 1kg Caster Sugar
- 1 x 10g Packet of Pectin
- 2 Vanilla Pods
- 1 Lemon

Method

1. Place the Rhubarb in a large, heavy-bottomed saucepan, along with the sugar and the vanilla pods (halved).
2. Heat everything on a low heat – stirring constantly until the sugar has completely dissolved.
3. Then, add a good squeeze of lemon juice and the pectin, still continuing to stir.
4. Increase the heat to a rolling boil, and skim off any scum which many rise to the surface.
5. Test the setting point (see *Temperature*), and if your jam has finished cooking remove from the heat.
6. Once it has cooled slightly, remove the vanilla pods (making sure the seeds are scraped out).
7. Pour your warm jam into warm, sterilised jars and seal. This Queen of conserves is now ready.

W IS FOR... WALNUTS

Walnut jam is very popular in France, but a relative rarity in England. This is a shame, because it really is a fantastic preserve which allows one to enjoy this nutrient-rich nut in a variety of ways. Try if you can to retain the texture of the walnuts, by not making your jam too fine and avoid over-indulging on the sugar. Less is more in this recipe. Walnut jam is delicious with vanilla ice cream (try half and half with the Rhubarb and vanilla jam above for a great topping), or as a filling for coffee cakes or macaroons. It is also lovely with cooked caramelized pears.... Be adventurous!

Walnut Jam

Ingredients

- 500g Cooking Apples
- 100g Walnuts
- 50g Butter
- 100g Muscovado Sugar
- 1 Lemon (zest and juice)
- 1 Bay Leaf

Method

10. Chop the apples into small chunks (keeping the peel for a more rustic jam) and place them in a large, heavy-bottomed saucepan with a little water.
11. Then, add the chopped walnuts, butter, sugar, lemon and bay leaf. Work quickly here, so the apples do not brown.
12. Bring everything up to a low-temperature and cook for about ten minutes (or until the apples are soft enough to prick with a fork).
13. Now, bring the temperature up and boil for a further five minutes, or until most of the liquid has evaporated.
14. Remove the bay leaf and leave the jam to cool slightly.
15. Pour the warm jam into warm, sterilized glass jars and seal. This jam can be eaten hot or cold.

X IS FOR... XMAS!

This is a lovely festive recipe, which uses the rich, ruby-red fruit; cranberries. Most widely used and grown in North America, cranberries are a fantastic little berry, rich in vitamins C, D, potassium and iron. They are also believed to be a natural remedy for a whole host of health conditions. Cranberries really do come into their own around Christmas, and cupboard would be complete without some homemade cranberry jam. As cranberries can be quite tart and sour, especially when under ripe, do feel free to add more sugar to this jam according to taste. Also, do experiment with the liquids you use (instead of water), apple juice or cider works well – as would a good helping of port.

Spiced Cranberry Jam

Ingredients

- 1kg Cranberries
- 600g Sugar
- 600ml Liquid
- 1 Lemon (Zest and Juice)
- 1 Orange (Zest and Juice)
- 2 tsp Cinnamon
- 1 tblsp grated Ginger
- A pinch of ground Cloves.

Method

1. Place the cranberries, sugar, orange, lemon – and whatever liquid you choose in a large, heavy-bottomed saucepan over a low heat.
2. Bring the mixture to the boil, and skim off any scum which rises to the surface.
3. Cook for roughly ten minutes, or until the cranberries are soft enough to squeeze against the edge of the saucepan with a fork.
4. Add the rest of the spices and continue to stir.
5. Cook your jam until it starts to thicken – at this point you should check its setting point (see **T**emperature). If it has got too thick, feel free to add more water.
6. If the jam has been cooked for long enough, take it off the heat and allow to cool slightly.
7. Pour your warm jam into warm, sterilised jars and seal. Your festive treat is ready!

Y IS FOR... YULETIDE

Here is another fantastic festive recipe. This spiced winter jelly uses a very traditional array of mulling spices – making it an exceptionally good accompaniment to a festive meat and cheese board. These spices are usually used to flavour drinks such as hot apple cider, mulled wine and wassail during the autumn and winter, but as is evident here, can be used for a whole array of purposes. The traditional definition of 'mulled' is a drink which has been prepared with these spices, usually through heating the drink in a pot and then straining. So here is your very own 'mulled jelly.' Enjoy - and feel free to add wine and cider to the recipe, as you see fit!

Winter Spiced Jelly

Ingredients
- 1kg Cooking Apples
- 400g Sugar
- 4 Leaves of Gelatine
- 100ml wine or cider vinegar
- 10 Cloves
- 7 Bay Leaves
- 4 Star Anise
- 4 Allspice Berries
- 2 Cinnamon Sticks
- 1 Tsp grated nutmeg
- 1 Orange / Lemon (for the peel)

Method

1. Soften the gelatine in a bowl of water and chop the apples (including the core and peel) into chunks.

2. Combine the apples, all the spices (save a few for decoration when the jelly is finished), peel and bay leaves into a heavy-bottomed saucepan.

3. Pour over enough water to cover and bring to the boil.

4. Then, turn down the heat and simmer with a lid or heavy plate on top for roughly one and a half hours.

5. Pour the mixture into a jelly bag, and leave to strain overnight (remember not to squeeze it through yourself, as this will result in a cloudy jelly!)

6. Once you have collected this liquid, pour it back into a heavy-bottomed saucepan, alongside the sugar and vinegar.

7. Cook over a very low heat until everything is dissolved, stirring constantly. Once fully dissolved, boil for just over ten minutes. Then add the gelatine and stir over a lower heat.

8. Now, test the setting point (see *Temperature*) and skim off any scum which may have risen to the surface.

9. Pour your warm jelly into warm jars, and add any spices which may make an elegant garnish. Once the jelly has semi-set, you can push these into the middle, so they are not just floating on the top.

10. Once your jelly is cold, it is ready to eat!

Z IS FOR... ZEST

Citrus fruits make wonderful-tasting jellies and marmalades, and this one will have the most gorgeous, vibrant colour thanks to the lemon's natural hue. This recipe for lemon marmalade is a classic recipe to master; slightly easier than the orange variant, because you can use a little more sugar. Once you have a supply of lemon marmalade, you will amazed at how many uses you will find for it. Not only can it be enjoyed as a normal marmalade on toast, but it's incredibly handy if you are making a lemon-drizzle cake; perfect added to toppings. This recipe uses the juice and rinds - really making the most of this wonderful fruit.

Lemon Marmalade

Ingredients

- 1kg (unwaxed) Lemons   - 2kg Granulated Sugar

Method

1. Wash the lemons and remove the top stalk.
2. Place them in a large saucepan with about two litres of water, and bring to the boil.
3. Simmer the lemons for two hours, or long enough so that the skins are soft (you can test by piercing the lemons with a fork).
4. Take the lemons out the pan, preserving the liquid, and allow the fruits to cool.
5. Then, cut the lemons in half and remove the pips and pith – saving them for later, (trying to reserve the juice!) and cut the lemon peel into strips – as thick or as thin as you like for the final marmalade.
6. Tie the pips and pith in a piece of muslin cloth.
7. Put all of this; lemon juice, rind and sugar, along with about half the cooking liquid back into the saucepan and boil rapidly for about twenty minutes.
8. Test the setting point of your marmalade (see *T**emperature*), and cook for longer if this point has not been reached.
9. When set, allow the mixture to cool slightly, remove the bag of pips, and skim off any scum which has risen to the surface.
10. Pour it into warm, sterilised jars and seal. Your marmalade is ready.

SERVING S

There are so many ways to serve jams and jellies, and hopefully we have given you some ideas with each recipe. The great thing about jams and jellies, is that they can be paired with savoury or sweet foods alike - think quince with cheese, blackberries with pork (instead of the standard apple sauce), cranberry with stuffing, raspberry with chocolate, elderflower with rhubarb and roses with delicate desserts. The list goes on. Try to think of the fruit or flavouring on its own, and what foods you would pair that with normally – and then exactly the same will apply to your jam or jelly! For the beginners, try experimenting by using a new flavour in a tried and tested recipe. Half the fun is in the trialling, so be brave...

As we've already noted, the wonderful thing about making your own homemade products is the fun one can have with creating customised labels and garnishes to the finished jars (think berries, citrus zest, herb sprigs). For the flower jams and jellies, a few fresh flowers are beautiful accompaniments - either inside the clearer jellies or scattered on top. Exactly the same applies

GGESTIONS

for the berries, fruits and spices; whatever main ingredient you have used, save some back for decoration afterwards. Jams and Jellies really do make the perfect vintage-inspired present as well as personal treat.

Make sure to source some lovely glass jars (kilner 'clip tops' work well, as do the traditional jam jar which you will find in most homeware stores). This will instantly make your creations look the part. As well as this, for serving jellies at dinner parties, there are so many wonderfully decorated and inventive moulds out there, so have a bit of fun! At this point, you can also make your own tags (think brown card and twine) to hang around the top of the jars, as well as handwritten labels to adorn the your containers. You could also place a little square of material ('gingham' is always lovely, though 'paisley' would also look a treat) over the top of your jar. Tied with some twine, this gives a great vintage-inspired twist to your presents, and we're sure the recipients will be touched by your efforts. Good luck, and happy decorating.

TEN TOP TIPS

1. Fruit should *always* be sound, ripe (or really, slightly under), but never *over-ripe* – clean and dry. Fruit picked in wet (or even continuously foggy weather) makes jam and jellies which will develop mould in a very short time.

2. For jams in general, fruit should be boiled gently until cooked - *before* the sugar is added, then boiled *fast* for a *short* time until it jells. The flavour will be more like fresh fruit if this method is followed. But if it is over-boiled *after* adding sugar, the flavour, colour and consistency will all suffer.

3. Always stir well until the sugar is dissolved! Additionally, a wooden spoon is best for *stirring* and a metal one to remove scum as it gathers.

4. Do not use *too* large quantities of fruit at a time – large quantities are extremely difficult to handle without the proper equipment.

5. A pinch of bicarbonate of soda, added to very sour fruits (such as lemon or gooseberry) counteracts the acid, and less sugar is required.

6. Always have jars warm, ready for your jams and jellies.

...AND TRICKS

7. The only exception to this above rule for jams is berried fruits – leave these until cool before putting into jars. This prevents berries from rising.

8. A great way to test the set of your jams and jellies is to put some on a cold plate – and when it has cooled, hold the plate vertical. If the jam remains on the plate it is cooked. If its on the floor – it isn't! This applies equally to jellies.

9. Store in a dry, cool place. The greatest enemies to jams and jellies are mould and crystallization. As long as they do not encounter any steam or heat after production, your products should keep for a very long time.

10. Do make sure your jars are properly sterilised, as the cleanliness of equipment is probably one of the most important factors in the shelf-life of your home-made jams and jellies.

BUT MOST IMPORTANTLY, JUST HAVE FUN!

Two Magpies

Copyright © 2013 Two Magpies Publishing

An imprint of Read Publishing Ltd
Home Farm, 44 Evesham Road, Cookhill, Alcester, Warwickshire, B49 5LJ

Commissioning Editor Rose Hewlett
Words by Amelia Carruthers
Design and Illustrations by Zoë Horn Haywood

This book is copyright and may not be reproduced or copied in any way without the express permission of the publisher in writing.

British Library Cataloguing-in-Publication Data A catalogue record for this book is available from the British Library.

www.ingramcontent.com/pod-product-compliance
Lightning Source LLC
Chambersburg PA
CBHW062122080426
42734CB00012B/2950